Laura and her little brother Ben lived with t[...]
right on the outskirts of a big cit[...]

One quiet evening, Laura and Ben put on their pyjamas, brushed their teeth and hopped into bed. On this particular night, as Laura struggled to fall asleep, she heard the pitter-patter of little feet scurrying on the ground.

SQUEA

"Ben, did you hear that?"
she whispered.
"No, I'm trying to sleep!"
groaned Ben. Laura laid
back down, tossing and
turning as she tried to
sleep. A few minutes
passed, when suddenly she
heard the noise again. She
quickly turned on her
bedside lamp and yelled,
"AHA!"

Ben sat up to see.
Between their beds stood
a chubby little mouse.

"Hi, I am Archie," said the mouse.
"Woah, you can talk!" Ben replied, as he and Laura stared at Archie in surprise.
"I'm here because we desperately need your help," Archie continued.
"Who's we?" asked Laura.
Archie replied, "Animals, well people too – in fact, the whole world! Can I show you both something?"

"This sounds important!" exclaimed Ben, who was now curious about what Archie wanted to show.
Suddenly, Archie flicked his tail, and the three of them were standing on ice at the North Pole.
"Woah!" said Ben and Laura with excitement. "Look, a polar bear!"

Ben took a few steps forward to get a closer look.
"I can see his ribs and he is losing his fur! What is happening?" Ben
asked, with sadness in his voice.
Archie responded, "You see, it is global warming. Humans for so long have
been polluting the Earth and now our wonderful planet is slowly dying."

"The ice is melting, and it is hard for animals like this polar bear to find food," he continued.
"This shouldn't be happening!" Laura cried.
"There is more that you both must see," replied Archie.

Archie flicked his tail once again, and in a flash, they arrived at the next destination. "Where are we? Why does everything look so...dry?" asked Laura, as she and Ben looked around. "We are in California, one of the many places taken over by drought. In places like this, there is too much heat and not enough water," Archie explained.

"Every year the climate sadly gets hotter and hotter. Wildfires have swept across many places in the world. The earth is burning, and we animals are dying very quickly," said Archie. "How is the world getting so hot?" asked Ben, trying to understand.

Archie looked at him and said, "Over a few hundred years, oil, coal and gas have been fueling people's homes and cars, as well as many factories. These fuels release a gas called carbon dioxide into the air which makes it hard for heat to escape our atmosphere, which is the bubble protecting Earth. With this trapped heat, the Earth gets hotter and hotter and it is becoming harder for many animals to survive."

Laura and Ben looked at each other with great disappointment in their eyes; Earth, the place they lived, the place they played, and the place they loved, was slowly dying.

Archie said, "I have one more place for you to see." He then flicked his tail again, and in a flash, they arrived at the oceans of Australia.

This is the Great Barrier Reef, which is full of many different species of coral. Did you know 25% of ocean life needs coral reefs to survive? Millions and millions of amazing sea animals rely on them for food, a home, and a place to raise their babies. The problem is that coral reefs need cold water to survive; however, due to climate change the water is becoming too warm.

"Here, put these on!" said Archie while he handed both of them flippers, goggles and an oxygen tank. They jumped into the ocean and followed Archie down to the coral reef.

Laura and Ben pointed at the beautiful reef and looked at each other in amazement, as it was unlike anything they had ever seen before. They were surrounded by the most colourful fish and beautiful coral.

Then Archie guided them further to a different reef. All the coral had turned white and all the beautiful fish and colours that they had just seen were not there. The reef was ruined.

When they got back onto the sand, Laura threw her goggles down in frustration and said, "I don't understand, why are we doing this? It's unfair for the Earth and it's unfair for the animals."
Ben asked Archie, "What can we do to help?"

Archie replied, "There are many things that all humans can do to help. For example, walking or riding a bike instead of using a car whenever possible.

Or, reusing things as frequently as possible so the factories who produce so much carbon dioxide can slow down. You could also choose to recycle things like paper, plastic and glass."

Archie continued, "There are also things you can do at home, such as drying your washing outside instead of using a tumble dryer.

Or, wearing a jumper when it is cold instead of turning on the heating.

Opening the windows instead of turning on the air conditioning in the summer can help.

Even unplugging electronics when you are not using them will help save the Earth."

We can all save our planet together if we choose
to change the way that we live.

For the last time, Archie flicked his tail and they all arrived back home. Ben and Laura now saw the world differently. From that day onwards they made changes to their lives because they realised how much they loved the Earth.